WEST COUNTRY COOKING

Cream

Michael Raffael

Supported by Objective
5b EAGGF Funds

HALSGROVE

Foreword

Arguably the most evocative writer about British cookery this century, Margaret Costa wrote: 'I use a lot of cream because I like very simple food.' She was reminding cooks that it suits pastoral, unpretentious cooking more than elaborate cuisine where its presence makes otherwise decent food over-rich.

As a cook, living on the borders of Somerset, Devon and Dorset, I use a little fresh cream a lot and a lot of cream once in a while. It goes into my scrambled eggs, custards, soups, sauces, on or in cakes, scones and berries. Mixed with fresh herbs, I add it to vegetables instead of butter. It softens the horseradish sauce with my Devon beef, enriches my junket and forms the basis of all my ice creams. It's truly an affordable luxury, as essential to my routine cooking as olive oil is to an Italian and far more versatile.

RECIPE PAGE 8

RECIPE PAGE 37

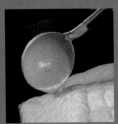

RECIPE PAGE 57

RECIPE PAGE 13

RECIPE PAGE 45

RECIPE PAGE 61

RECIPE PAGE 23

RECIPE PAGE 49

RECIPE PAGE 55

RECIPE PAGE 69

Contents

Foreword 3

Cream Teas 7

Cream Past 19

Cream at War 31

Creme de la Creme 39

Cream Cocktail 51

Ice Cream 65

Appendix 72

Acknowledgements 74

Suppliers 74

Recipe Index 77

Cream Teas

'Nowhere is the English genius for domesticity more notably
evidenced than in the festival of afternoon tea.'

George Gissing

'There are few hours in life more agreeable than the hour
dedicated to the ceremony known as afternoon tea.'

Henry James

Clotted Cream

Don't be fooled. There is no difference between Devonshire and Cornish clotted cream. It's a myth that was started over half a century ago when the two counties were vying with each other to capture their shares of summer holiday-makers.

However, as early as the turn of this century, there were four separate ways of preparing it. The best and the oldest which has been used in farmhouses for at least 400 years is to stand milk, fresh from the cow for up to 18 hours, then pour it into a shallowish container and heat it very slowly (according to folklore a peat fire was best) until a thick creamy skin formed on top. This was skimmed off. Really skilled dairy maids were able to cut it and roll it up like a swiss roll.

The other ways were all attempts at speeding up and industrializing the process. Either the milk was passed through a separator and the cream poured on top, or the setting time was accelerated. What happens more often nowadays is that only the separated cream is scalded which can make the end result taste a little like condensed milk. Also, it is not unusual for manufacturers to scald the cream in plastic containers. This, some experts claim, leaves an uncharacteristic after-taste which is not for purists.

Clotted cream is very rich and wicked, a gallon of milk yields about 12 oz (350 g), but until recently it was considered a positive health benefit. The New Health Society, dedicated to improving the nation's health after World War I, claimed 'Clotted cream is now largely recommended by the medical profession as an excellent fatty food and is displacing to some extent the use of cod liver oil.'

Judges at agricultural shows in the West look for the following qualities when assessing clotted cream:

- **Full nutty flavour**
- **A characteristically wrinkled appearance**
- **Moderately thick texture**
- **Straw colour is sometimes preferred**

Faults are: too smooth (a sign of acidity and poor flavour), cheesy texture, oiliness or softness.

Only those with easy access to the freshest raw milk should attempt to make their own clotted cream. Five litres (1 gallon) should produce about 500 g (1 lb). Pour the new milk into a large, shallow pan, preferably stainless steel and leave to stand in the refrigerator for at least 12 hours. Warm the milk to 85 C. Keep it steady at this temperature for 45 minutes to an hour (Aga and Rayburn users tell me that they sometimes have to leave it up to two hours). Leave it to cool for 12 to 16 hours, the longer the better to obtain a firm, crisp skin. Cut the cream around the sides of the pan and use a sharp-edged perforated skimmer to remove the clotted cream.

Scones

It's better to make scones with plain flour and a measure of baking powder, than to rely on SR flour. The dedicated home baker will prepare his or her own baking powder from 2 parts cream of tartar to one part bi-carb, because modern proprietary brands use phosphoric acid which, though highly effective, leaves a faint after-taste.

Makes 12 to 18, depending on size
60 g softened butter
50 g caster sugar
150 ml tepid full-fat milk
240 g plain flour
15 g baking powder
beaten egg, flour, or milk for the tops

Preheat the oven to 225 C, gas mark 7. Cream the butter and sugar either by hand or in a food processor. Incorporate half the milk (don't worry about curdling). Sift the flour and baking powder twice. Add to the creamed mixture and start to work in. Pour in the rest of the milk and work the dough until smooth. (Add a little extra flour if it seems too sticky.) Don't over-blend or over-knead. Roll out to 2 cm thick for larger scones or 1.5 cm for tea scones. Cut out with a fluted 5 cm or 6 cm cutter. Put on a baking sheet. Either glaze the tops with beaten egg or milk or dust with flour. Bake for approximately 15 minutes.

Strawberry Jam

Strawberry jam starts in the field or kitchen garden. If you don't pick your own, making it is a hit and miss affair. Pick the fruit ripe and after a dry spell. Leave the stalks attached. Don't bruise the berries. Different varieties go in and out of fashion; most are suitable for jamming.

Makes about 3.5 kilos
2.3 kilos strawberries after removing stalks
2 kilos granulated or preserving sugar
Optional: 3 tablespoons lemon juice

Wash the strawberries (despite what some books say) rapidly under cold water, drain them and remove the stalks without pulling out the plugs along with them. Put the fruit into a large, preferably stainless steel pan, pour over the sugar and leave to stand overnight or for five or six hours. Turn on the heat and stir the strawberries till the sugar dissolves. Add lemon juice if you use it. Boil rapidly to 105 C, measured with a cooking probe or sugar thermometer. Skim off any scum on the surface. Pour the jam into prepared jars.

To prepare recycled jars: wash thoroughly both jars and lids. Stand both upside down to dry. Put them on a tray and warm them in a very low oven (125 C, Gas Mark 1/2) for 20 to 30 minutes. Pour the jam into the hot jars and seal at once.

Note: strawberry jam should not require any pectin to set it

Geraldene Holt's Devonshire Honey Cake

Food writer and potter, Geraldene Holt, who spent many years in Cullompton, included this cake in *A Cup of Tea*, a celebration of early Minton tea cup patterns. Honey cakes still figure regularly in baking competitions held at West Country shows and fetes. Hers, beautifully moist, almost like a Parkin, and intensely flavoured is worthy of a prize.

Serves 8

170 g runny Devon honey
150 g butter
80 g light muscovado or soft brown sugar
1 tbsp water
1 large beaten egg
200 g SR flour, sifted with an extra teaspoon of baking powder

Line and grease a 22 cm [7 inch] baking tin. Preheat the oven to 180 C, gas mark 4. Melt the honey, butter, sugar and water in a pan over a low flame. Beat in the egg and then the flour. Turn the mixture into the tin and bake 40 to 45 minutes until the cake is springy in the centre and the edges are just shrinking from the tin. Cool in the tin one minute and turn on to a wire rack.

Mrs Holt likes to put a little honey glaze over the cake while it's still warm. Combine a tablespoon of warmed honey, 60 g icing sugar and 2 tablespoons of water and brush over cake.

Thunder and Lightning

Splits or Chudleighs, belong to the Billy Bunter epoch when no afternoon tea worthy of the name was complete without its cream bun.
According to a 1922 WI cookery book thunder and lightning are 'splits
eaten with treacle', but Golden Syrup is better. You can, of course, buy
plain buns instead of making your own providing that you warm them
in the oven before serving.

Serves 8
300 g strong white flour
150 ml warm milk (37-43 C)
1 dessert spoon quick acting yeast
40 g castor sugar
1/2 teaspoon salt
30 g lard
1 small beaten egg
icing sugar
250 g clotted cream
Golden Syrup

Put the flour in a low oven for 10 minutes. It should feel warm to the
touch. Combine the milk, yeast, sugar and salt. Rub the lard into the
flour. Pour over the liquid and mix thoroughly so that the flour is
thoroughly moistened. Knead, either by hand or in a machine until a
smooth elastic dough forms. Cover with cling film and leave to double
in volume. Knock out the air. Divide the dough into eight pieces, roll
them into balls and arrange them on a baking sheet. Brush with beaten

egg. Leave them to rise again and bake 12-15 minutes in a preheated oven 220 C, gas mark 7.

Now, here's the trick! The crust should be be soft, so when the buns come out of the oven wrap them in a thick cloth (old recipes specify a blanket) and leave them to cool down. Then while they are still warmish, dust with icing sugar and make a split through the top of the buns. Fill with clotted cream and drizzle syrup over the top.

Note: in her Book of English Food, *Arabella Boxer, suggests that Devonshire Splits are 'crisp', so if you prefer them this way you don't have to swaddle them after baking.*

Sandwiches

'English tea sandwiches are dainty affairs. They should be cut very thin with a sharp knife, trimmed of crusts or not, and cut in half or four. Day-old bread, white or wholemeal, makes cutting easier. Butter lightly and fill generously.' Claudia Roden, *Picnic* (Penguin).

Instead of sliced factory bread, buy a good quality loaf from a craft baker. It will slice more easily if it has been left in the freezer until almost frozen, but not solid.

'There is nothing more relishing than a really good sandwich. Unfortunately, at some of the buffets, at restaurants and railway stations, they do not bear the best of reputation.' C.H. Senn, *Recherché Side Dishes*, 1899.

Charles Senn's Superior Sandwich Butter

'Weigh half a pound of butter and work it in a basin with a wooden spoon until soft, then add gently a gill of whipped cream, a little salt and mustard to taste... it is more convenient for spreading and the sandwiches eat far better than those made with ordinary butter.'

To prepare cucumber for sandwiches: peel, slice finely, sprinkle with salt and leave in a colander to drain. Rinse, pat dry, season and flavour with a little lemon juice or diluted malt vinegar.

Velvet Chocolate Torte

Aga expert and television cook, Mary Berry, learnt her craft at Bath's College of Domestic Science. She remembers being taught to prepare food in pairs with one student playing the cook's role and the other the house maid's. She bought her cream then (the 1950s), from Hands Dairy in York Street. Various types were kept in huge china bowls and ladeled out into cartons by weight.

Serves 12
2 x 100 g bars Bournville plain chocolate
100 g caster sugar
6 tablespoons water

4 egg yolks
2 tablespoons brandy
560 ml (1 pint) double cream

Break the plain chocolate into squares and drop them in the processor. Process one minute until a few raisin-sized pieces remain in the powdery chocolate. Put the water and sugar in a pan, dissolve and boil three to four minutes to obtain a syrup. turn on the processor and pour the hot syrup over the chocolate so that it melts the chocolate. Add the eggs, then brandy and continue processing until very smooth and silky. Whisk the cream until it has plenty of volume but is not yet stiff. Incorporate the chocolate base and turn the mixture into a spring-form tin (or a bowl if you aren't worried about presentation). Freeze about three hours till set, but not hard. The texture is very suave. Remove from the tin.

To serve, dust a medium sized plate with icing sugar. Arrange a wedge of the torte on top with strawberries or other fruit around it and dribble a little single cream over the top.

Note: other spirits or liqueurs can be used instead of brandy. Ginger is especially good.

Cream Past

'...a clout is a thick patch, presumably leather, since you have old shoes unclouted – and the cream wrinkles up into leathery folds.'

Dorothy Hartley

'The old spellings give "clowtyd, clouted, clowted, clawted and clotted", we presume the cream was the same thick, wrinkled, folded, yellow, crusted cream as made by the country people today.'

Dorothy Hartley

Junket

Junket, or juncade as it was originally known, used to be made in a rush basket and it was sometimes served on a rush mat. It was closer to a fresh cream cheese than the fragile curd which it later became. When it has been properly made, it should cut into smooth shiny slices like jelly. It can be made plain, flavoured simply with sugar – milkmen once delivered it like this to doorsteps in the days when yoghourt was considered to be a strange foreign aberration – but it's better for being flavoured with cinnamon and brandy.

Serves 4

600 ml Jersey milk or Devon if you have a farming friend
1 heaped tablespoon caster sugar
1 tablespoon brandy
pinch of powdered cinnamon
5-6 drops vegetarian rennet diluted with a dessertspoon of
boiled cooled water
clotted cream

Warm the milk to blood temperature. Add the sugar and dissolve it. Stir in the brandy, cinnamon and rennet. Stir well. Pour into a bowl or four individual serving dishes. Leave to set at room temperature. Accompany with clotted cream, dusted with a little extra cinnamon. Plain junket is very good eaten with a puree of fruit: strawberries, greengages or raspberries.

Damask Cream

An enriched junket made with a blend of single and double cream instead of milk, flavoured with rose water and served in a bowl set on a flat dish on which deep red scented rose petals were strewn was popular in fashionable Bath during the eighteenth century.

Syllabub

The syllabub topping for Martha Bradley's trifle (below) contains no alcohol. It was known as an Everlasting Syllabub to contrast it with the fragile froths of cream which were whipped up under the watchful gaze of a cow and drunk like milkshake. The best loved recipes though, are alcoholic. There's even a proverb attesting to the fact: a syllabub without brandy is like kissing a man without a moustache.

Serves 6
grated zest of 2 lemons
80 ml medium sherry
juice 1 lemon
2 tablespoons brandy
1 pint double cream
60 g caster sugar

Combine the ingredients, whisk until firm and chill for 2 hours.

Martha Bradley's Trifle

Mrs Martha Bradley, late of Bath, wrote one of the great early books on food, *The British Housewife* (c.1765). She divided it into chapters corresponding to the months of the year, thereby creating the first truly seasonal cookery book. She gave advice on choosing 'fresh Provisions' as well as recipes for cooking them.

'Break into a large bowl some naples biscuits, macaroons and ratafia cakes. Cover the bottom of the bowl with these and pour over as much sack as will just wet them through. Make a boiled custard, but more thick; set it by to cool and when quite cold, pour it over them; and then pour in a syllabub over that and garnish with currant jelly and ratafia cakes.'

Serves 6-8
500 ml whole milk
8 yolks
220 g caster sugar
30 g cornflour
vanilla essence
4 roughly chopped macaroons
30 ratafia biscuits
1 packet sponge fingers
150 ml Bristol Cream sherry
2 tablespoons brandy

300 ml double cream
grated zest and juice 1/2 lemon
60 g red currant jelly

Boil the milk. Whisk the yolks, half the sugar, cornflour and vanilla till smooth. Pour over milk. Combine thoroughly. Return to the heat and stir till the custard thickens and boils. Set aside. Put macaroons, 15 ratafias and sponge fingers in a trifle bowl. Moisten with the sherry and brandy. Whip the cream with the rest of the sugar, lemon zest and juice until it forms a stiff peak. Spoon the custard over the biscuits in the bowl. Leave it to cool. Pile the whipped cream on top. Boil red currant jelly till runny. Let it cool till almost set. Fill a mini-piping bag with it and drizzle over the cream. Decorate with the rest of the ratafias.
The red currant jelly isn't really necessary. In any case, when Mrs Bradley was cooking it would have looked more like Rowntree's Fruit Pastilles. Her contemporaries decorated trifles with candied violets and rose petals. Lemon zests are an easy alternative.

Frumenty

'Mrs Tanser of the St James Hotel, Henry Street, Bath says her mother who owned a dairy farm near Chipping Sodbury used to prepare frumenty as a cold sweet for Mothering Sunday with eggs and fruit, but added a little cream. She put it in china bowls and sent it to her best customers.' Florence White, *Good Things in England* (1932).
Frumenty has been around since the Middle Ages and was once the

West's most popular sweet. It has become almost extinct, probably because it's prepared over two days rather than the two minutes it takes to whizz up an Instant Whip. It has a unique texture, vaguely like a very creamy rice pudding and tastes as rich and fruity as plum pudding.

Serves 10-12
450 ml whole milk
110 g Bulgar wheat
50 g currants
30 g sultanas
3 tablespoons rum
500 ml single cream
lemon zest
100 g honey
mixed spice

Boil the milk, rain in the wheat, cover and leave in a warm place overnight, during which time the wheat will swell up and become glutinous (it's sometimes called creed at this stage). Soak the currants and sultanas in rum. Mix the cream with the wheat, add lemon zest, honey and spice and cook gently over a low flame till creamy. Blend with a food processor (a modern heresy, but it improves the texture) add a little extra milk if necessary. Stir in the fruit and rum. Turn into individual bowls and serve cold.

Black Treacle Cream

This is a 'modern' cousin of the stone cream family. It comes from Angela Rawson who for many years owned the Loaves and Fishes at Wootton Bassett. It dates from the 1970s when cream flowed through the arteries of most restaurateurs.

Serves 4
3 eggs (yolks and whites separated)
50 g caster sugar
2 tablespoons water
2 tablespoons treacle
3 teaspoons gelatine dissolved in hot water
220 ml whipping cream

Whisk the yolks and sugar till creamy, then beat in the water and treacle. Stir in the melted gelatine. Whip up the cream till it has plenty of volume and is about the same texture as the treacle mix and fold it into the treacle. Whisk the egg whites till firm and fold into the treacle. turn into a bowl or individual glasses and leave to set. Decorate with cream, chopped nuts or candied violets.

Stone Creams

In the days before refrigerators were invented, Stone Cream was a kind of rich milk jelly, given this name because it was taken down into the cellar and left on cold flagstones to set. In 1865, Mrs E. Wallas Matthews, married to the manager of a webbing factory in Crewkerne wrote *My Madeira Cookery Book*, based on her experiences living on the island, because, she complained, West Country women 'are rarely skilled in more than the every-day plain dinner art (and that is but seldom done well).' Her recipes are mainly Portuguese: mackerel soup, Jao Quintal's famous pudding, tangerine preserve, but she also describes several creams including a crema de jinja.

Serves 4
250 ml single cream
5 egg yolks
30 g sugar
50 g syrup from a jar of preserved ginger
1/2 sachet of gelatine dissolved in 60 ml hot water
100 ml whipping cream
30 g caster sugar
rose petals
2 pieces of preserved ginger

Bring the cream to the boil in a small pan. Whisk the yolks, sugar and syrup. Pour over the cream, blend well. Return to the pan and heat without boiling till it coats the back of a wooden spoon. Stir in the gelatine. Pour into individual glass dishes. Put in the refrigerator to set. Whisk the whipping cream and sugar. Fold in rose petals very carefully. Pile on top of the creams if they are individual servings. Decorate with finely shredded slivers of ginger.

Celia Fiennes Apple Pie

While she was travelling around England on horseback in 1695, Celia
Fiennes stopped at a small market town in Cornwall, known as St
Austell:

> '*Here was a pretty good dining room and chamber within it
> and very neat country women. My landlady brought me one of
> the West Country tarts; this was the first I met with
> though I had asked for them in many places in Somerset and
> Devonshire. It is an apple pie with a custard all on top.
> It is the most acceptable entertainment that could be made
> me. They scald the cream and milk in most parts of these
> countries, and so it is a sort of clouted cream, as we
> call it, with a little sugar, and so put on top of the
> apple pie. I was much pleased with my supper.*'

Serves 6
250 g flour
75 g softened butter
60 g shortening (pastry fat)
55 ml milk
500 g peeled and cored cooking apples
2 cloves
grated zest of 1/2 lemon
optional: 60 g chopped quince
120 g sugar
2 eating apples

1 tablespoon semolina or ground rice
beaten egg yolk
250 g clotted cream mixed with a tablespoon caster sugar

Put the flour in a mixing bowl, add the chopped fats and rub in with fingers until crumbly. Pour on the milk and work the dough into a smooth ball. Divide the pastry into two: one for the base of the pie and the other for the lid. Roll out the base and line a greased 20 cm (8 inch) pie ring. Roll out the pastry lid and reserve.

Put the cooking apple, cloves, lemon and optional quince in a pan with a tablespoon of water. Cover and stew till soft. Empty the apple onto a sieve above a bowl so any excess juices drain off. Transfer to a bowl and add 100 g sugar and the peeled, cored and diced eating apples.

Preheat the oven to 190 C, gas mark 5. Sprinkle semolina over the pastry base. Add the apple. Fit the pastry lid. Make a hole in it for the steam to escape. Decorate with pastry trimmings. Brush with egg and dust with the rest of the sugar. Bake 40-45 minutes. Accompany with a blob of lightly sweetened clotted cream.

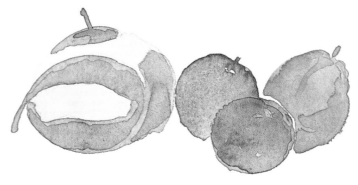

Cream at War

'Did you know,' ran a reader's letter in **Woman** *during the period of rationing after the war, 'that a delightful substitute for cream can be made by adding a mashed banana to the white of an egg?'*

From *Four Seasons Cookery* by Margaret Costa

Cornish Cream, by Phyllis Nicholson, described the austerities of wartime England and particularly her work cooking in a Cornish NAAFI for newly mobilised troops. One evening, she was invited for high tea at a friend's farm where she was able to forget rationing:

> *'The meal is laid. White china on a blue cloth. A great black kettle bubbles on the fire. Bits of brass gleam about the walls. The floor is stone, mighty flags grooved with the passing of the years. Mrs Jolly is broad and welcoming. We eat scrambled eggs, coarse brown bread, gooseberry tart and clotted cream, followed by tea in large, thick cups.'*

Scrambled Eggs

A Welsummer hen's egg, has a dark lustrous shell, stippled with dark brown freckles. Its yolk is a thick golden yellow, the white like a clear glaze. A gulf separates eggs from chickens which run around the farmyard from mass produced ones, be they battery or nominally free-range. To eat scrambled eggs with real eggs is a luxury. To make them properly requires skill, patience and a decent, thick-based pan.

Serves 3-4
60 g butter
8 eggs
salt
freshly milled white pepper
100 ml approx. double cream

Warm a pan over the lowest possible setting on the range. Add the butter and let it melt without sizzling. Beat the eggs, salt and pepper together so that they are thoroughly blended, but not frothy. Pour into the pan. Work them around in the pan stirring constantly till they are just set and soft curds are forming. Take the pan off the heat and beat in the cream. This reduces the temperature of the eggs and stops them from overcooking. The finished texture should be light and moist not over-coagulated and hard.

Scrambled eggs have been used in the Regional Finals to determine France's best apprentice chef, so don't underestimate the difficulty.

'Coarse Bread'

When World War II broke, white bread was the norm and the National Wheatmeal Loaf introduced to replace it seemed like a poor substitute. Mrs Jolly's 'coarse bread', would probably have been made with what we know today as brown flour, which contains 85% of the wheat berry with a little of the outer husk removed.

500 g brown flour
1 heaped teaspoon salt
10 g lard
Optional: 1 teaspoon treacle
1 heaped teaspoon dried yeast
300-330 ml water at 40 C

In winter warm the flour in a very low oven 10 minutes. Sift flour and salt into a large mixing bowl. Rub in the lard and treacle if you use it. Dissolve the yeast in water. Pour the water onto the flour. Mix in, then knead till smooth, about 10 minutes. Cover with a cloth and leave to rise in a warm place until it doubles its size. Knock back the dough. Take it out of its bowl and knead it into shape. Put it into a greased baking tin. Cover it again. Leave it to rise a second time. Preheat the oven to 200 C, gas mark 6. Bake the loaf 45 to 50 minutes, turn out on to a cooling wire and leave to cool.

Home baked brown bread often seems either too dense or too crumbly. When the dough has risen the first time, divide it into two pieces, roll each one into a ball and lay them side by side in the tin. This makes the bread more springy.

In winter add an extra pinch of yeast.

'Making Tea'

'This is one of the things that must be done very swiftly. If you are making tea to carry in on a tray, put everything ready first – cups, bread and butter, cakes, biscuits, milk, sugar. Fill the kettle fresh from the cold water tap; never use hot tap water. When it boils, pour some into the pot and make it very hot. Add a little more to the kettle, and by the time it boils your pot will be hot. Empty the water out, put in the tea and pour on the water at once. Take it straight into the room and use it at once. Tea that stands in the pot is injurious to the digestion and very unpleasant in taste.'

Leonora Eyles, *Eat Well In War-Time*

Mock Cream!

'Condensed milk was useful for making sweets, cake fillings and mock cream. The Ministry of Food recommended whipping it up with gelatine and fruit juice, coffee or chocolate flavouring.'

From The Wartime Kitchen Garden, by Jennifer Davies

Makes about 1 pint
1 can condensed milk
1 sachet gelatine
To flavour:
fruit juice, cocoa powder,
or vanilla flavouring

Open the can of condensed milk. Pour the gelatine into a small measuring jug and add about 150 ml of cold water. Stand in a pan of hot water until the gelatine has dissolved (don't stir). Spoon the milk into a mixing bowl and mix in the dissolved gelatine. Whisk until the mixture becomes light and frothy.

Now fold in your flavouring to taste with a metal spoon and leave the mixture to set in a cool place, the larder or pantry.

Note: the mixture could be used on scones, to fill cake or as a kind of milk jelly by itself.

Author's note: This recipe comes with no guarantee.

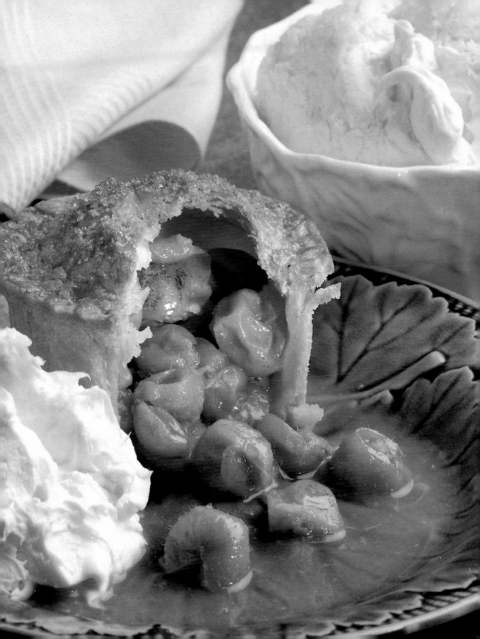

Oldbury Tarts

Whether the Gloucestershire village of Oldbury or its namesake in
Warwickshire gave birth to these little gooseberry pies is unclear, but
Kenneth Bell, a famous restaurateur of the 1970s revived them at
Thornbury Castle.

Serves 4

200 g flour

salt

1 yolk

100 ml water

75 g butter

350 g top and tailed green or yellow gooseberries

120 g demerara sugar

Serve with 150 g clotted cream

Generously grease four ramekins (size 2 dl). Sift flour and salt and mix
in the yolk. Boil water and butter in a pan. Beat in the flour till smooth,
turn onto a work surface and cool. Divide into four. Roll out and line
the ramekins, keeping back trimmings for the pastry lids. Fill the
pastry with gooseberries and all but 20 g. of sugar. Roll out the trimmings and fit the lids on the pastry. Seal well. Make a hole in the tops
to let the steam escape. Brush the top with water and sprinkle the rest
of the sugar on top. Bake one hour in a preheated oven at 170 C, gas
mark 3. Cool, turn out and serve while still warm (although cold is
fine), by loosening the pastry edges with a thin-bladed knife, tilting
slightly and tapping the bottoms.

Creme de la Creme

'Cream is one of the most necessary and worthwhile of little luxuries.'

'Eggs and cream go together like buttercups and daisies.'

'Too much cream is a sign of vulgarity in restaurant cooking and of ignorance at home.'

From *Four Seasons Cookery* by Margaret Costa

Fillets of Sole from Padstow

'*This is fillets of sole with tiny mussels from the bays around Padstow, in a sauce made from the local farmhouse cider, mussel juice, clotted cream from a farm at Trevone and maybe flavoured with chopped chives from my garden.*' Rick Stein, *English Seafood Cookery*.

Serves 4
40 small mussels
90 ml dry cider
4 x 90 g skinned fillets Dover sole
60 g clotted cream
10 chives cut diagonally into 5 mm lengths

Preheat the oven to 180 C, gas mark 4. Wash the mussels in several changes of water, place them in a saucepan with some of the cider and open them over a high heat with the lid on. As soon as they have opened, empty them into a colander with a bowl underneath to collect the cooking juice. Remove the beards from all mussels and discard shells of all but 16.

Put the sole fillets in a shallow buttered cooking dish and pour a little of the mussel cooking liquor over them; cover with buttered paper and poach in the oven till just cooked through (about 5 minutes). Pour the cooking liquor into a small saucepan and add the mussel liquor, the rest of the cider and the clotted cream. Bring to the boil and reduce by rapid boiling till the sauce coats the back of a spoon. Put the 24 shelled and 16 unshelled mussels and the chives in with the sauce and warm through. Put the fillets on four warmed plates and pour the sauce and the mussels over them.

Note: you can achieve the same result with double cream.

———————————

Baked Brill with a Clotted Cream Sauce

For over 15 years I've bought fish from the Newton family which owns a small fish shop on the beach at Beer in South Devon. They sold me monkfish and John Dory for 30p per pound at a time when chic restaurants had barely heard of them and never served them. Brill look like turbot, but they are less gnarled and their heads not so lopsided.

Serves 4
1 x 1350 g brill
115 ml dry cider
220 g leek
50 g butter
2 peeled Cox's apples
115 g sliced mushrooms
2 tablespoons Somerset cider brandy
350 ml clotted cream
salt and pepper

Cut off the fish head, fins and tail. Put them in a pan with the cider. Boil, simmer and strain after 20 minutes. Preheat oven to 230 C, gas mark 8. Cut the leek into postage size pieces. Lightly butter a dish or shallow-sided tin, large enough to hold the fish. Spread leeks over it, with the fish on top black skin down. Add stock. Put quartered apples round it. Season. Bake about 15 minutes, basting twice. Heat the remaining butter, saute the mushrooms in it and season. Heat and flame the brandy in a small pan. Pour it over the fish. Lift it out on to a serving dish. Strain the liquid into a frying pan, reduce to about 150 ml. Beat in the clotted cream, but don't boil it. Add leek, apple and mushrooms. Adjust seasoning. Pour over the fish or serve individual fillets and pour sauce over them.

Pan Fried Squab Breasts with Brandy and Cream Sauce

According to teacher and writer Caroline Yates rough shooting is a Boxing Day tradition in the Vale of Pewsey: 'The bag will include wood pigeon. It's very easy to pluck; but in this instance you remove the skin and feathers together making it even easier. Cut out the breasts and make some stock with what's left, to use for the sauce.'
In Wilts 'Squab' refers either to the weakest bird of a brood or the runt of a litter of pigs, but in Devon squabs (meaning young pigeons) used to be kept tied to their nest so that the parents went on feeding them till they were plump enough to eat.

Serves 2
15 ml oil
40 g butter
salt and pepper
4 plump pigeon breasts
120 g finely diced onion
125 ml brandy
80 ml pigeon stock
1 tablespoon white wine vinegar
300 ml double cream

Heat the oil in a frying pan. When it's hot add the butter. Season the pigeon breasts and brown in the pan on both sides (but don't cook through). Remove from the pan and reserve. Stir in the onions and cook till soft and starting to brown. Pour in the brandy and flame. Add the stock. Reduce the liquid to a glaze, scraping the pan with a spatula. Add the vinegar and cream. Reduce the sauce to a rich coating consistency. Check the seasoning. Return the pigeon to the pan long enough for it to heat through.

Warm Goat's Cheese and Hazelnut Tart

When he introduced this recipe in *A Pinch of Salt*, Stephen Ross of the Queensberry Hotel in Bath wrote: 'Instead of slaving over a hot stove for twenty years, we should have been breeding goats, as the popularity of goat's cheese seems boundless.' Goat's cheese is now being made throughout the West with some of the best coming from Mary Holbrook's Sleight Farm, Timsbury.

Serves 8
butter for greasing
220 g good shortcrust pastry
6 free range eggs + 3 yolks
300 ml double cream
150 ml milk
220 g fresh goat's cheese
salt, pepper and grated nutmeg
50 g chopped, toasted hazelnuts

Grease a deep-sided flan dish (25 cm). Roll out pastry very finely and line dish. Chill thoroughly. Preheat the oven to 180 C, gas mark 4. Bake blind 15 minutes and cool. Blend remaining ingredients bar the nuts, pour into the part-cooked flan case and bake 30 minutes. Check the top it shouldn't be too brown. Cover with foil if it is. Continue baking till set. Sprinkle the nuts over the top.

Baked Egg Custard Tart with Nutmeg Ice Cream

Kit Chapman, doyen of the Castle Hotel Taunton has led a one man crusade to promote the concept of Modern British Cooking. He gave Gary Rhodes his first big break when he employed him as chef and introduced him to television.

Phil Vickery, Mr Chapman's current chef, is every bit as talented and won an Egon Ronay award for this exquisite pudding.

Serves 4-6

6 egg yolks

60 g caster sugar

1 level tsp cornflour

500 ml whipping cream at boiling point

dash of rose water

1 x 15 cm baked pastry case

(sugar or short crust, rolled thin)

250 g best quality vanilla ice cream

nutmeg

Preheat the oven to 170 C, gas mark 3. Whisk the yolks, sugar and cornflour until creamy. Pour on the boiling cream, mix thoroughly and strain through a fine sieve. Flavour with rose water. Pour into the pastry case and bake till set. Cool.

Spoon the ice cream into a food processor. Grate nutmeg into it.

Process rapidly to blend in the spice. Serve the custard with a large lozenge of ice cream.

Note: Phil Vickery accompanies the tart with a blackcurrant sauce: puree 150 g stewed blackcurrants with 40 g sugar, a squeeze of lemon juice and about 100 ml water. Sieve and chill.

Rich Baked Egg Custard

A simple variant on Phil Vickery's tart, this requires very rich well-flavoured eggs to do it justice.

Serves 4
2 tablespoons milk
400 ml whipping cream
4 egg yolks (larger the better)
60 g caster sugar
vanilla essence
butter

Brush a saucepan (not aluminium) with milk. Pour in the cream and heat to boiling point. Preheat oven to 150 C, gas mark 1. Whisk the eggs, caster sugar and vanilla essence. Mix in the cream. Butter a 15 x 5 cm approx pie dish and stand it in a tray of hot water. Strain the eggs-cream mixture into the pie dish. Put it in the oven and bake till just set, about 50 minutes. Eaten hot it is very delicate, but allowed to cool it becomes the texture of a crème brûlée. It's good with a red fruit puree.

Lemon Cremets

Joyce Molyneux, mistress of the Carved Angel, Dartmouth started her career at the Hole in the Wall, Bath, run by a restaurant pioneer, George Perry-Smith who introduced the cooking of Elizabeth David to the dining-out public. One of the most popular desserts then, she recalls, was cremets: 'George found this wonderful source of unpasteurized cream on a farm near Castle Cary. It was probably illegal to use it, but I've never found anything as good since.'
Cremet moulds are heart shaped and have holes in the bottom.

Serves 8
250 ml single cream
250 ml double cream
60 g caster sugar
juice and grated zest of a lemon
2 egg whites

Whip the creams together with sugar and lemon till soft and fluffy. Whisk the whites till they form stiff peaks and fold into the cream. Line cremet pots with muslin and spoon the cream into them. Fold muslin back over the cream and stand them on a rack. Leave them overnight. Turn out and peel away muslin. Accompany with poached peaches, soft fruit or a fruit puree.
Note: if you don't have the right mould, pierce small plastic containers with a skewer.

Cream Cocktail

'I could also point out, though that the French have one of the lowest rates of heart attacks in the world. And we all know how they like their dairy produce.'

Nigel Slater

'Never add cream to a large amount of boiling liquid. Take a little of the hot liquid and mix with the cream first, then add the cream gently off the heat. Once the cream has been incorporated, the liquid can be boiled safely. When adding cream to juices in the frying pan to make a sauce, gradually stir in the cream off the heat, then bring to the boil.'

Lynda Brown, *The Modern Cook's Manual.*

New Potato and Cream Pasties

The recipe for this unusual pasty comes from Mrs Margaret Toller of Helston. 'I was born,' she writes, 'in Morwenstow, near Bude, Cornwall. My mother made the pasty when new potatoes were available. People who live near me have never heard of it. The only person who has done came from Fowey. As my maternal grandmother came from Portloe, perhaps that's where it came from.'

Makes 4
500 g white bread flour
110 g lard
110 g chilled hard margarine or butter
175 - 190 ml water
1 kilo scraped and sliced new potatoes
250 g clotted cream
salt and plenty of black pepper
1 beaten egg yolk

Rub half the lard into sifted flour and salt. Slice in the remaining fats. Mix roughly with knife. Add water and work into a smooth ball. Rest 30 minutes. Preheat oven to 200 C, gas mark 6. Divide pastry into four, roll out 4 x 20 cm circles and moisten the edges. Pile potato into the centre of each one. Add a large dollop of cream, season. Lift the edges and crimp firmly together. Make a hole for steam to escape. Brush with egg yolk. Put on a greased baking tin and bake 15 minutes. Reduce to 150 C, gas mark 1 and bake 45 minutes more. 'Handsum!!'

Eltrot Soup

In *Wiltshire Cookery*, cooks and authors Angela Rawson and Nikki Kedge note: 'Eltrot is an old Wiltshire word for the wild parsnip which can still be found on waste ground and grassy places. The roots should be washed, peeled and boiled till quite soft, about $1/2$ hour, then mashed and pressed through a sieve to remove fibrous parts.' The taste resembles the cultivated variety so it's not cheating too much to make their soup with these.

Makes 2.5 litres
80 g unsalted butter
6 small parsnips, peeled and chopped
2 large onions, chopped
1 crushed garlic clove
3 teaspoons curry paste
1 litre chicken stock (or vegetable)
salt and pepper
150 ml single cream

Melt the butter in a heavy duty pan, add the parsnips and onions, cover and cook over a very low flame till softened. Stir in the garlic and curry paste. Cook for a minute, then pour over the stock. Simmer 20 minutes and season. Liquidize, add the cream and check the seasoning again. Reheat, but do not boil.

Swede and Saffron Soup

Part of the West Country Cooking initiative begun in 1996 was to collect hundreds of authentic recipes from the Six Counties.
This elegant soup with strong Cornish overtones was sent in by Esme Francis of St Just.

Makes 2.5 litres
60 g unsalted butter
450 g swede - peeled, sliced thin
250 g chopped white of leek
250 g chopped onion
170 g chopped celery
1.2 litres chicken stock
2 bayleaves
8 parsley stalks
1/2 teaspoon dried thyme
8 saffron threads
150 ml double cream
salt and pepper

Melt butter in a pan, add the vegetables, cover and sweat over a low heat for 10 minutes. Add the stock, bayleaves, parsley and thyme. Simmer 30 minutes. Discard bayleaves and parsley, then liquidize the soup. Put the saffron in a mortar, pour over a tablespoon simmering water and roughly pound. Add the saffron and its water to the soup. Leave 10 minutes. Stir in the cream, bring back to simmer and season.

Tamar Salmon and Sorrel Sauce

Chef and author Sonia Stevenson is a mistress of the art of saucing.
For 20 years, with her husband Patrick she ran the Horn of Plenty at
Gulworthy overlooking the Tamar Valley. There she kept her own
chickens, cultivated a flourishing kitchen garden and possibly broke the
law by making junket with unpasteurized milk from a neighbouring
farm. She also went out foraging for wild food including the sorrel to
accompany salmon which swim up the Tamar. In the West it's a year
round herb,whereas the cultivated variety is more tender and seasonal.

Serves 4
100 g butter
2 large handfuls of sorrel
or 3 in winter when sorrel is milder
300 ml double cream
salt and pepper
900 g middle cut salmon on the bone
(or 4 x 150 g skinned fillets)

Melt 60 g butter in a pan. Add the sorrel and cook till it wilts and turns
khaki. Puree the sorrel and season. Put the sorrel in a small pan, add
the cream and boil to a light coating consistency. Check seasoning. and
reserve.
Remove the fillets from the bone. Pull out any pin-bones with a pair of
tweezers. Remove the skin with a flexible, sharp-bladed knife. Slice
each fillet in two so that you halve the thickness. Put each fillet between

cling film and flatten slightly. Season. Heat the remaining butter in a large non-stick frying pan. Fry about 30 seconds on one side and 20 seconds on the other (do the fillets one at a time if you are worried about your reactions and dexterity).

Arrange the fillets on individual plates and spoon the sauce over them. Sonia Stevenson suggests that you go on a sorrel hunt (it grows on pastureland and in hedgerows) and prepare a large batch of the puree which can be stored successfully in jars for several weeks, or frozen.

Dippie

The W.I. has, more than any other agency, been working to protect folk cookery. This oddity is from *Cornish Recipes* (1929) when pilchards still swam around the South West coast.

'Boil potatoes and pilchards in thin cream or dippie.
This dish is called 'Dippie' and was very popular before
cream was demanded by the factories.'

Gratin of Shellfish and Oyster mushrooms

Serves 4
175 g oyster mushrooms
50 g butter
16 mussels
1 tablespoon dry white
4 scallops, shelled
300 ml double cream
50 g grated mature cheddar
1 teaspoon arrowroot
1 tablespoon medium sherry
salt, pepper
115 g shelled prawns

Slice oyster mushrooms and fry in butter over a high flame so they colour rapidly (do not let the butter burn). Remove from the pan. Add the mussels and wine to the pan and place over a high heat until they open. Take them out and reserve. Add scallops and cook for 3 minutes, turning after a minute or two. Take them out of the pan. Add cream and reduce it till it starts to thicken. Stir in the cheddar. Dissolve arrowroot in sherry. Whisk into the sauce. Adjust the seasoning. Take mussels from shells. Put them with scallops, prawns and oyster mushrooms in ovenproof dish. Pour over the sauce and flash under a hot grill to brown.

Burrow Hill Pheasant

James, under-gamekeeper at Midelney Manor emerges from the cling-ing mist of the Somerset Levels with a buzzard on his shoulder and carrying a brace of pheasants. He's delivering them to Julian and Diane Temperley on their cider farm at Kingsbury Episcopi, near Taunton. The Temperleys have been the driving force behind the revival of Somerset cider brandy. This is the key ingredient in Mrs Temperley's pheasant dish which she has evolved from an early Keith Floyd recipe.

Serves 6
200 g butter
salt and pepper
2 drawn pheasants
120 ml Somerset cider brandy
450 ml Burrow Hill dry cider (or similar scrumpy)
6 peeled, cored and halved eating apples
120 ml double cream

Heat 100 g butter in a large flameproof casserole. Season the pheasants inside and out. Brown on all sides in the hot fat. Discard the fat which will have burnt. Pour over half the brandy and flame. Pour over the cider. Fry the halved apples in the rest of the butter in a separate pan. As soon as they are coloured add them to the casserole with the pheas-ants. Cover and simmer on top of the stove or in a moderate oven 190 C, gas mark 5 for 40 minutes. Take the pheasants and apples from the casserole. Keep hot. Reduce the liquid in the pan to a glaze. Stir in the cream. Boil till lightly thickened and add as much of the remaining cider brandy as is to your taste. Joint the pheasants, arrange on a serving dish with the apples and pour over the sauce. Serves 4-6. Note: Instead of cooking the apples with the pheasants, they may be added at the end as a garnish.

Strawberries and Cream

In a field, strawberries warm with the afternoon sun on them taste better than those picked on a cold dank morning. So, when serving them at home, they should never be left to chill in a fridge. It is, however, a good idea to cut them up a little and sprinkle sugar on them about an hour before you intend eating them. The sugar dissolves with the juices, rather than remaining on the surface of the fruit.

200 g strawberries per person
caster sugar
80 ml double cream per person

Halve the strawberries or quarter very large ones, dust with sugar and leave one hour, not much longer or they will start to look tired. Serve and pour over cream.

In the Latin countries cooks sometimes squeeze lemon or orange juice over stawberries, a kind of homeopathic culinary practice. It's nice for a change, but if the fruit is fragrant and perfectly ripe it doesn't improve them.

Wiltshire Elderflower Fritters

Philippa Davenport, *Country Living's* favourite daughter, lives near Marlborough. From her farming neighbour, Mrs Wooton, who kept a house cow, she learnt how to make these fritters. They resemble the wafer-thin pancakes known as Quire of Paper in early 18th century cookery books. This modern version is adapted from Michael Smith's classic *Fine English Cookery*.

Serves 4
100 g flour
pinch of salt
2 small eggs and two yolks
25 g caster sugar
150 ml single cream
130 - 150 ml full fat milk
elderflowers
unsalted butter for frying

Sift the flour and salt twice. Whisk eggs and sugar till it dissolves. Beat in cream and milk. Incorporate liquid into flour to obtain a thin, light dropping consistency. Take a fork and 'comb' elderflowers into batter. Rest 30 minutes. Heat a little butter in a frying pan (max. 20 cm) and fry pancakes keeping them as fine and fragile as possible. Stack them to keep hot. Serve dusted with sugar and whatever filling you like
Note: In the old Quire of Paper recipe, the filling was interspersed between pancake layers and the whole pile cut into wedges like a cake.

Ice Cream

Ice cream man on a Cornish beach 1940:
'The cart is white with gay green-gold lettering and
snowy-coated attendant. The incredible fat pony, whose
staple diet from his approach must be Cornish cream, has
the calm nature that invariably accompanies
deeply covered ribs.'

Phyllis Nicholson, *Cornish Cream*

Honey Ice Cream

Joyce Molyneux, of the Carved Angel, Dartmouth deserves to be
designated a National Treasure for her services to British cookery over
30 years. For this ice cream, she buys honey from a beekeeper in
Blackawton who produces several uniflora varieties including heather
which is best for this recipe.

Makes 1.25 litres
4 split green cardamoms
600 ml whole milk
175 g heather honey
4 egg yolks
300 ml double cream

Put the cardamoms in a pan with the milk and bring it to the boil.
Whisk the honey and yolks in a bowl and pour on the milk. Set the
bowl over a pan of simmering water (bowl mustn't touch water) and stir
until the custard coats the back of a wooden spoon. Remove from the
heat and strain to remove the cardamoms. Cool. Mix in the cream and
churn till frozen in an ice cream machine.

At the Carved Angel, this ice cream is often served with chilled pink
cantaloupe or charentais melons.

Note: If you don't have an ice cream maker, put the mixture in the freezer.
As it sets, beat with a fork or whisk to break down ice crystals at hourly
intervals.

Popham's Blackcurrant Ice Cream

Popham's began life eleven years ago as a take-away food shop in Winkleigh. The partners, Melvyn Popham and Dennis Hawkes then graduated to serving lunches of soup or cottage pie. Their culinary ambitions grew and their 10 seater restaurant serves some of the best lunches in Devon. Melvyn was born in the town. Denis ran the local Red Lion. They buy as much produce as they can from friends living close by. The blackcurrants for this recipe come from Melvyn's cousin Sonia, who lives in the neighbouring village of Hollacombe.

Makes about 1 litre
450 g washed blackcurrants
225 g caster sugar
60 ml Creme de Cassis
4 separated eggs
100 g icing sugar
270 ml double cream

Cook the blackcurrants in a very little water and sugar till tender. Sieve, add the Cassis and then chill. Whisk the egg whites adding the icing sugar gradually to form a shiny meringue. Stir in the yolks. Whip the cream till it has roughly the same texture as the meringue and fold it in. Fold in the blackcurrant puree. Transfer to a freezer till frozen. *Note: you don't need a machine to make this.*

Strawberry Clotted Cream Meringue Ice Cream

Rocombe Farm, near Torquay, has a unique claim to fame as an ice cream maker. Since it began almost 10 years ago, it has attempted over 2500 different varieties. This one, however, comes from owner Peter Redstone's own kitchen, based on the clotted cream he makes on the family's Aga.

Makes about 1.25 litres
170 g strawberries
1 tablespoon lemon juice
150 g caster sugar
4 eggs
220 ml Jersey or other rich milk
450 g clotted cream
1/2 cup of broken meringues (home made or shop)

Wash and puree the stawberries with a tablespoon of sugar and lemon juice. Whisk the rest of the sugar and eggs till creamy. Heat the milk and cream together to 70 C, stirring from time to time. Beat a cup of the mixture into the egg yolks. Empty the yolk mix into the cream/milk. Stir over a very low flame till the custard thickens slightly and coats the back of the spoon. Cool. Stir in strawberry puree. Empty into an ice cream maker and churn. Just before it sets fold in the meringue and leave to finish freezing.

Brandy Snap Baskets

Melt 70 g golden syrup, 40 g caster sugar, 70 g unsalted butter in a pan.
When it boils beat in 40 g flour, a splash of brandy, a pinch of ginger
plus a tablespoon of lemon juice with a teaspoon of grated zest. Cool.
Divide into 8 – 10 small balls. Lay them well apart from each other on a
greased baking sheet or silicone paper and flatten. Bake till melted and
bubbly at 170 C, gas mark 3 about 10 minutes. Shape around a tumbler
while still hot. Spoon ice cream into baskets when cooled

Clotted Cream Ice Cream

This is just about the richest ice cream ever. It comes from Wayne
Pearson at the Well House, St Keyne, near Liskeard.

Makes about 1.25 litres

6 yolks

200 g caster sugar

150 ml milk

1 vanilla pod

350 g clotted cream

300 ml double cream

Whisk yolks and sugar till they whiten. Put the milk and split vanilla
pod in a pan and boil. Leave to stand 5 minutes. Pour over the yolks
and combine well. Return to the pan and heat till it coats the back of

the spoon but don't boil. Take out the vanilla pod. Empty the custard into a mixing bowl. Whisk till cool. Incorporate the clotted cream. Stir in the double cream and transfer to the ice cream maker. Churn and eat as fresh as possible

---

Whortleberry Ice Cream

Whortleberries grow on heathland: Dartmoor, the Quantocks, the Blackdown Hills, but they take ages to pick even if you choose your moment well - a kind of a comb was the instrument favoured in the old days. They are related to blueberries, but smaller and more tart.

Makes about 1.25 litres
450 g whortleberries
juice of half a lemon
170 g caster sugar
250 ml whipping cream
250 ml double cream

Pick over and wash the fruit. Drain and leave to dry. Blend with a food processor adding lemon juice and sugar. Beat creams into the puree. Churn in the ice cream maker until almost frozen (-13 C) and serve at once, while still fresh and creamy

Note: without a machine, mix puree with creams, put in freezer. After an hour scrape frozen parts from the edges to the centre. Repeat till the ice cream is almost solid and then blend with a hand-held food processor.

71

Appendix

The most detailed early account of clotted cream making was described by a farmer, William Ellis in *The Country Housewife's Family Companion* 1750. He attributes it to 'a correspondent at Stowford, near Ivybridge'.

'The morning's milk is commonly set over the embers about four o'clock in the afternoon; but this varies according as they have more or less embers in a right heat, for many will set their milk over them as soon as they have done dinner, as there is commonly a good quantity of them free of smoke, and are ready without the trouble of making them on purpose: the evening's milk is commonly set over them about eight o'clock next morning, sooner or later; however care must be taken not to do it before the cream is well settled on the milk, which will be in the before-mentioned time. And as to the quantity of the milk we scald at once, it is very different: from one gallon in a pan to three or more; and the measure of each pan of the biggest size is three gallons or three and a half. There are pans of several sizes less, but the most common quantity is about two gallons, or two and a half in each brass pan; and brass pans are commonly used for this purpose, as they are certainly the best of all other inventions, because the milk will both heat and cool sooner, and far more safe than in the earthen sort; for these (especially in the summer time) are too long in cooling; and as the cream cannot be used before it is cold, these earthen pans are in disuse. I never saw any of them used in this manner but at Sir John Roger's: their reason was, that they are somewhat sweeter than brass pans, and I must confess they are so, if the brass ones are not kept in the nicest order possible. As to the height of the pans standing above the embers, it is according to the height of it on a trivet, which is commonly about six inches, with this difference; if on a stove six inches, if on a hearth eight inches, the latter being most in use. As to the exact time of scalding the milk, to have a full clouted cream on it, it is about one hour, yet this varies according to the heat of the embers, and therefore it is sometimes two or more hours, but seldom less than one. However, a moderate heat is best for rising the thickest cream ; and you may easily discover when it is scalded enough by a little swelling of the cream, and then it must be immediately taken off the fire. That which is scalded in the morning must be skimmed in the evening; and that in the evening or afternoon the next morning, with the hand only. When they have little to scald at once, they save several meals together, and then scald it; but this does not make the best butter. When they have no embers they use clean dry wood to burn under the pans, but they always refuse to burn rotten wood because it is apt to give an ill taste. The chimney must be kept very clean from soot, lest any drop into the milk. Sometimes when the pans are not very clean, they rub them with bayleaves (or in case they are very bad, they boil the leaves in the water they wash and scour the pans with) for these leaves are great sweeteners and cleansers and should be frequently used for this purpose, especially in the summer time.'

73

Acknowledgements

Cream would not have been possible without the help and support of many lovers of the West Country and its cooking. They include Albert Beer, Mary Berry, Kit Chapman, Philippa Davenport, Esme Francis, Anthony Gibson, Geraldene Holt, Tom Jaine, Nikki Kedge, Margaret Kelland, Diane Lethbridge, Joyce Molyneux, Wayne Pearson, Melvyn Popham, Antoinette Raffael, Angela Rawson, Peter Redstone, Stephen Ross, George and Amanda Streatfield, Richard Stein, Sonia Stevenson, Diane Temperley, Margaret Toller, Philip Vickery, Caroline Yates.

Suppliers

CORNWALL
Clotted Cream

B & A Lake,
Priors,
Coads Green,
Launceston, PL15 7LT
01566 782547

A & M Pigott,
East Penrest,
Lezant,
Launceston PL15 9NR
01579 370270

S. Jelbert,
9 New Road, Newlyn,
Penzance TR18 5PZ
01763 66634

Pengoon Farm,
Nancegollan,
Helston TR13 0BH
01326 561219

A.E.Rodda & Son,
The Creamery, Scorrier,
Redruth,
01209 820526

George Trenouth,
Trevone Farm,
Trevone,
Padstow.
01841 520489

Trewithen Farm Foods,
Trenithon Chancelor,
Probus,
Truro TR2 4HQ
017126 882205

Ice cream

Callestick Farm Dairy Ice Cream,
Callestick,
Truro TR4 9LL
01872 573126

Helsett Farm,
Helsett,
Lesnewth,
Boscastle, PL3 5HP
01840 6207

S. Jelbert,
9 New Road, Newlyn,
Penzance TR18 5PZ
01763 66634

DEVON
Clotted Cream

Langage Farm,
Plympton, PL7 5AW
01752 337723

Mrs A.E. Huxtable,
Town Living,
Stockleigh,
Pomeroy,
Crediton EX17
(24 hours notice needed)
01363 866248

Margaret Kelland,
North Horridge Farm,
Stoke Rivers,
Barnstaple
01271 850587

Village Farm,
Holne, TQ13 7SL
01364 631532

Ice Cream

Devonshire Farmhouse Ice Cream,
Higher Murchington Farm,
Chagford, TQ13 8HJ
01647 433648

Newton Ice Cream,
Old Newton Road,
Heathfield,
Newton Abbot TQ12 6RL
01626 835268

Pure Jersey Ice Cream,
Rookbeare Farm,
Cheriton Fitzpaine,
Crediton EX17 4BE
01363 866424

Rocombe Farm Fresh Ice-Cream,
123 Union Street,
Castle Circus,
Torquay TQ1 3DW
01803 293996

Salcombe Dairy,
Salcombe TQ8 8DX
01548 843228

The Big Sheep,
Abbotsham,
Bideford EX39 5AP
01237 472366

Thorn Farm,
Thorne Manor,
Pakrasweek,
Holsworthy EX22 7JD
01409 253342

DORSET
Clotted and other creams

Blackmore Vale Farm Cream,
Wincombe Lane,
Shaftsbury SP7 8PJ
01747 851855

SOMERSET
Clotted and other creams

Tower Farms, Deans Cross,
Lydeard St Lawrence,
Taunton TA4 3QN
01984 667252

Childhay Manor,
Crewkerne Business Park,
Blacknell Lane,
Crewkerne TA18 7HJ
01460 77422

Elliscombe Farm, Holton,
Wincanton BA9 9EA
01963 32393

Laurelbank Dairy,
14 Queen St,
Wells BA5 2DP
01749 679803

Ice Cream

Childhay Manor,
Crewkerne Business Park,
Blacknell Lane,
Crewkerne TA18 7HJ
01460 77422

Barnard and Gooding,
Keward Farm,
River Road, Pawlett,
Bridgwater TA6 5SE
01278 685173

WILTSHIRE
Cream

Berkeley Farm Dairy,
Wroughton,
Swindon SN4 9AQ
01793 812228

Recipe Index

Baked Brill with a Clotted CreamSauce 41

Baked Egg Custard Tart with Nutmeg Ice Cream 46

Black Treacle Cream 26

Brandysnap Baskets 70

Burrow Hill Pheasant 61

Celia Fiennes Apple Pie 28

Charles Senn's Superior Sandwich Butter 16

Clotted Cream 8

Clotted Cream Ice Cream 70

Coarse Bread 33

Damask Cream 21

Dippie 58

Eltrot Soup 53

Fillets of Sole from Padstow 40

Frumenty 24

Geraldene Holt's Devonshire Honey Cake 13

Gratin of Shellfish and Oyster mushrooms 59

Honey Ice Cream 66

Junket 20

Lemon Cremets 49

Matha Bradley's Trifle 23

Mock Cream! 35

New Potato and Cream Pasties 52

Oldbury Tarts 37

Pan fried Squab Breasts with Brandy and Cream Sauce 42

Popham's Blackcurrant Ice Cream 67

Rich Baked Egg Custard 47

Sandwiches 15

Scones 10

Scrambled Eggs 32

Stone Creams 26

Strawberries and Cream 62

Strawberry Clotted Cream Meringue Ice Cream 69

Strawberry Jam 11

Swede and Saffron Soup 55

Syllabub 21

Tamar Salmon and Sorrel Sauce 57

Thunder and Lightning 14

Velvet Chocolate Torte 16

Warm Goat's Cheese and Hazelnut Tart 45

Wiltshire Elderflower Fritters 63

Wortleberry Ice Cream 71

First published in Great Britain in 1997
Copyright © 1997 Michael Raffael

British Library Cataloguing-in-publication Data
CIP Record for this title is available from the British Library
ISBN 1 874448 07 8

HALSGROVE
Publishing, Media and Distribution
Halsgrove House
Lower Moor Way
Tiverton, Devon EX16 6SS
Tel: 01884 243242 Fax: 01884 243325

Design & Art Direction Andrew Sutterby
Photography Sam Bailey
Illustrations Moish Sokal

Printed in Italy by Tipolitografia Petruzzi Corrado + C.

Notes

Notes